FOR ORGANS, PIANOS & ELECTRONIC KEYBOARDS

E-Z PLAY TODAY

85

COWBOY SONGS
20 CLASSIC SADDLE SONGS

CONTENTS

ISBN 978-1-4234-0990-8

HAL•LEONARD®
CORPORATION

7777 W. BLUEMOUND RD. P.O. BOX 13819 MILWAUKEE, WI 53213

Visit Hal Leonard Online at
www.halleonard.com

Abilene

Registration 4
Rhythm: Swing

Words and Music by Lester Brown,
John D. Loudermilk and Bob Gibson

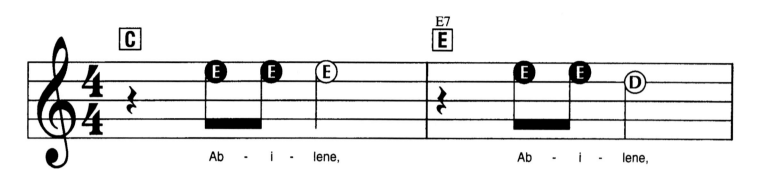

Ab - i - lene, Ab - i - lene,

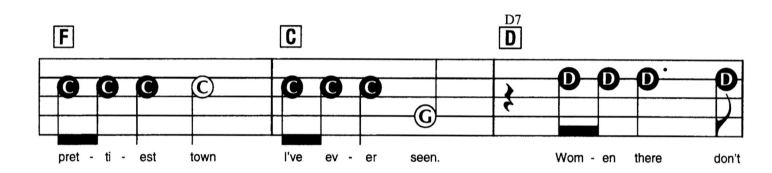

pret - ti - est town I've ev - er seen. Wom - en there don't

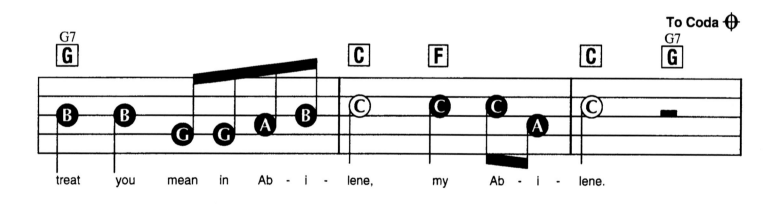

treat you mean in Ab - i - lene, my Ab - i - lene.

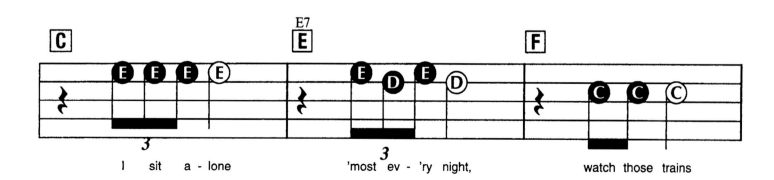

I sit a - lone 'most ev - 'ry night, watch those trains

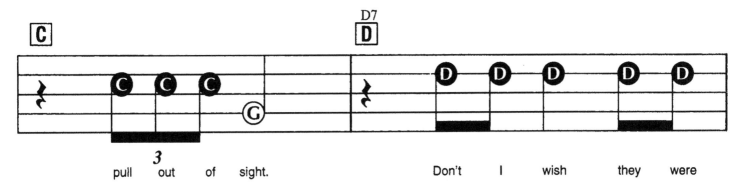

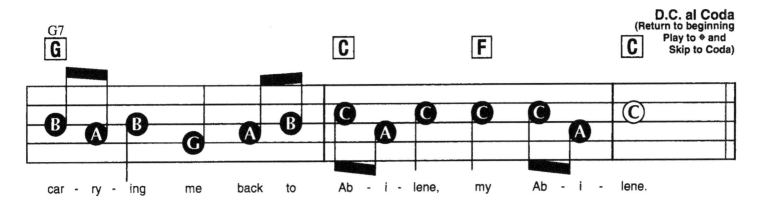

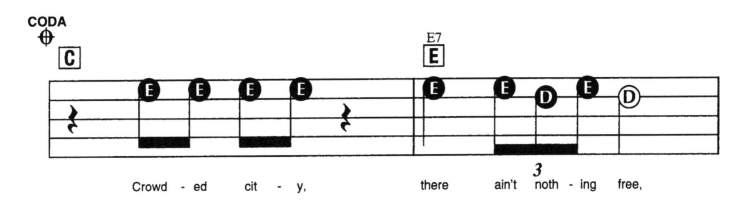

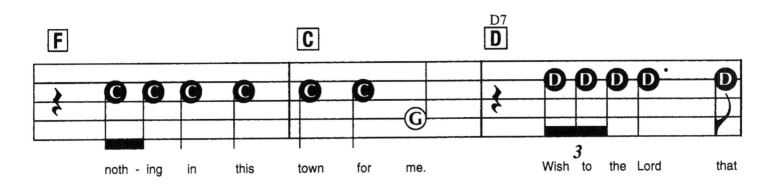

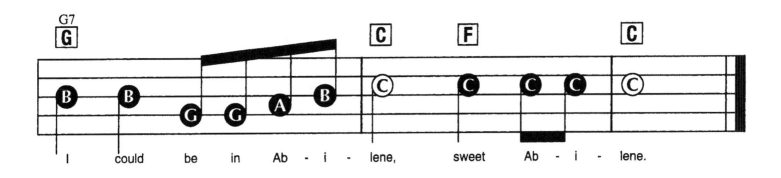

Along the Navajo Trail

Registration 4
Rhythm: Country Swing or Fox Trot

Words and Music by Dick Charles,
Larry Markes and Eddie De Lange

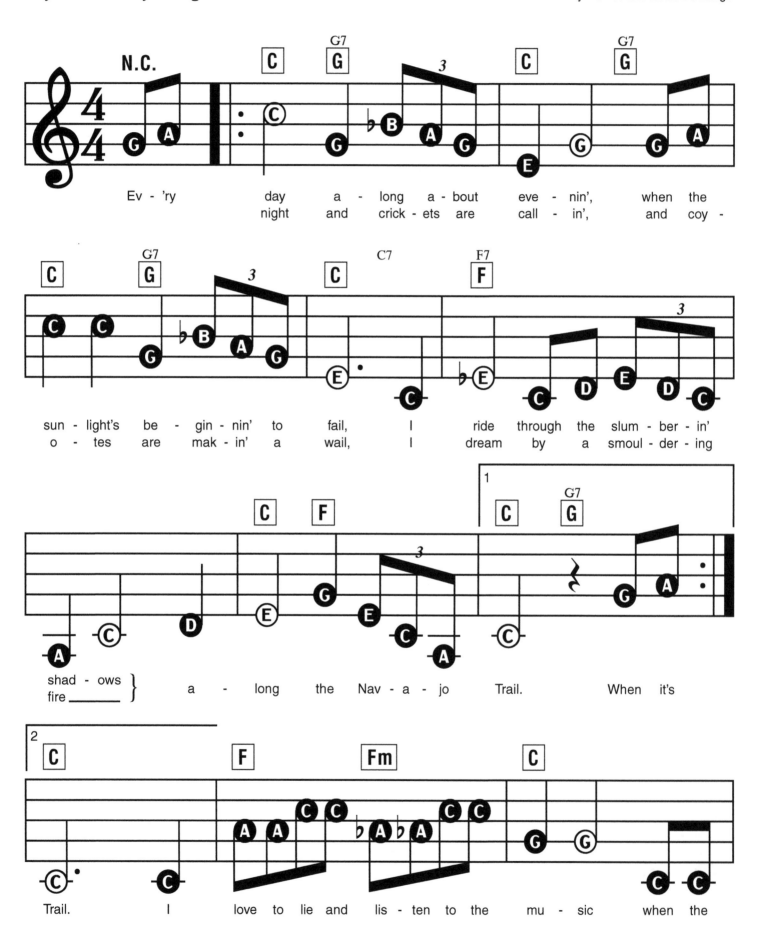

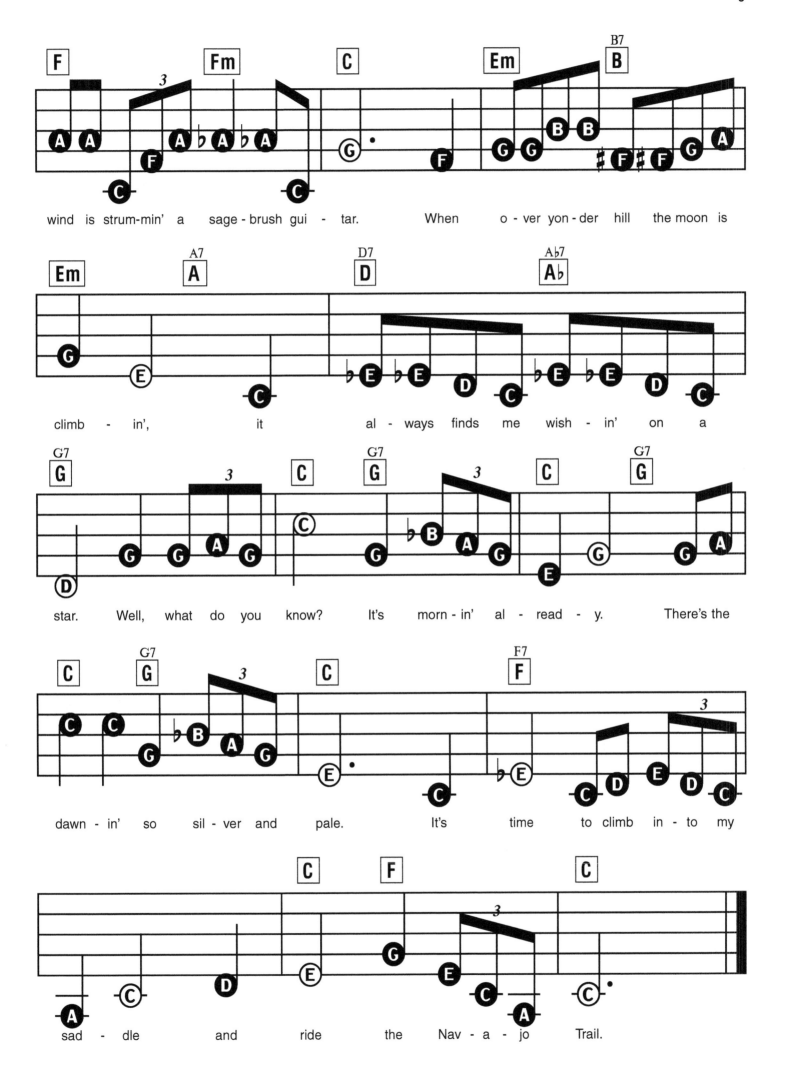

Back in the Saddle Again

Registration 1
Rhythm: Country Western or Fox Trot

Words and Music by Gene Autry
and Ray Whitley

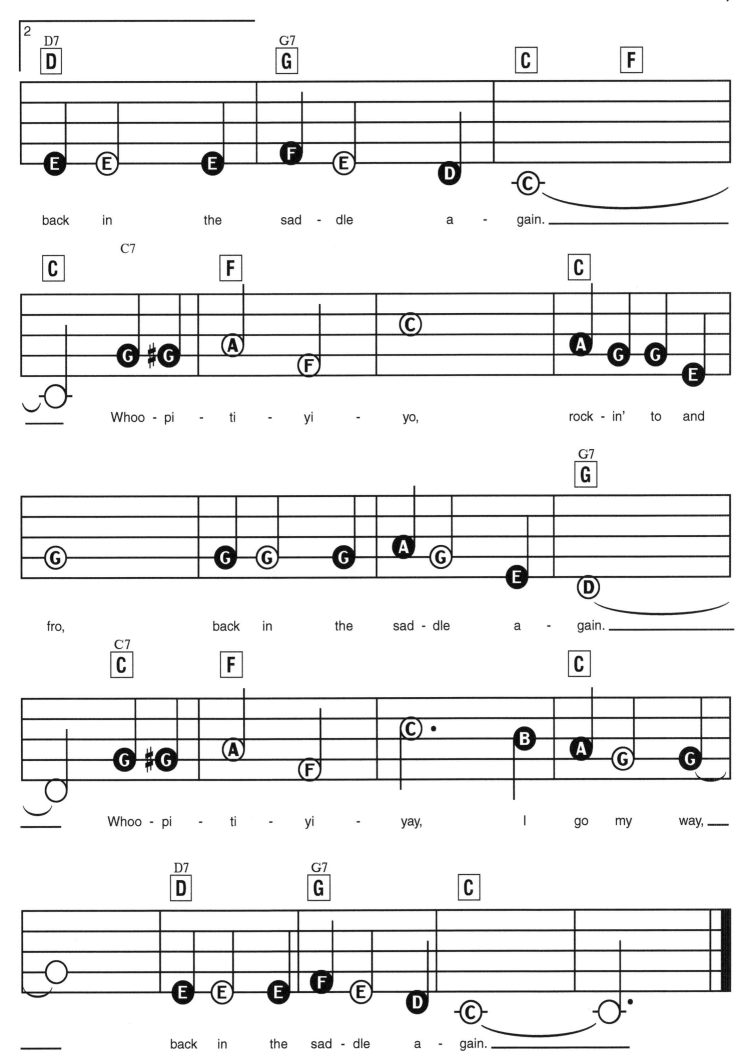

Bury Me Not on the Lone Prairie

Registration 4
Rhythm: Country or Fox Trot

Words based on the poem "The Ocean Burial" by Rev. Edwin H. Chapin
Music by Ossian N. Dodge

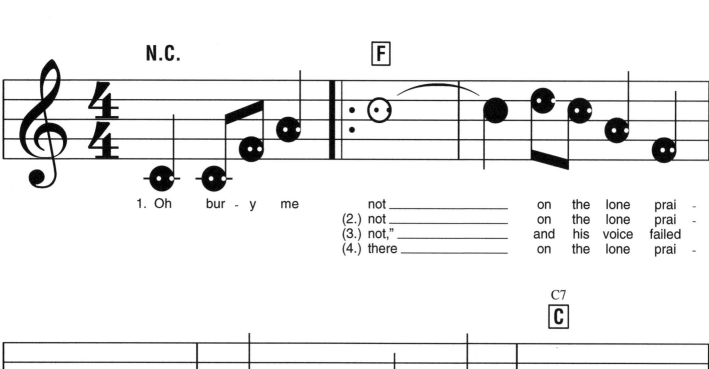

1. Oh bur - y me not _____ on the lone prai -
(2.) not _____ on the lone prai -
(3.) not," _____ and his voice failed
(4.) there _____ on the lone prai -

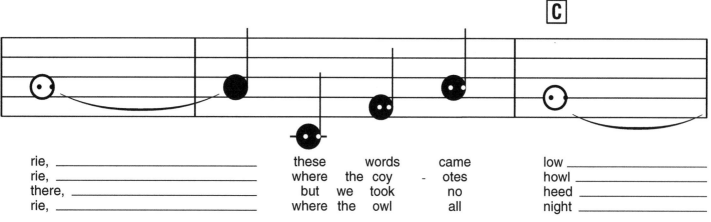

rie, _____ these words came low _____
rie, _____ where the coy - otes howl _____
there, _____ but we took no heed _____
rie, _____ where the owl all night _____

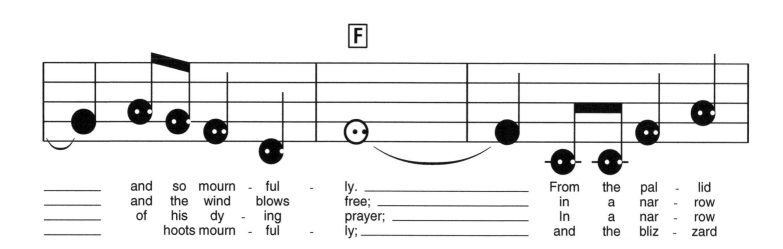

_____ and so mourn - ful - ly. _____ From the pal - lid
_____ and the wind blows free; _____ in a nar - row
_____ of his dy - ing prayer; _____ In a nar - row
_____ hoots mourn - ful - ly; _____ and the bliz - zard

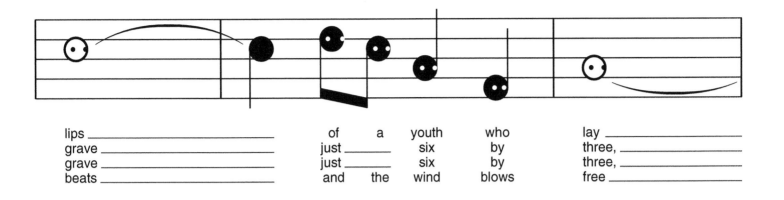

lips _____ of a youth who lay _____
grave _____ just _____ six by three, _____
grave _____ just _____ six by three, _____
beats _____ and the wind blows free _____

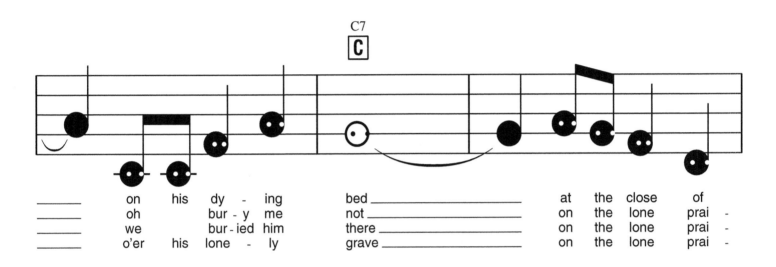

C7
C

_____ on his dy - ing bed _____ at the close of
_____ oh bur - y me not _____ on the lone prai -
_____ we bur - ied him there _____ on the lone prai -
_____ o'er his lone - ly grave _____ on the lone prai -

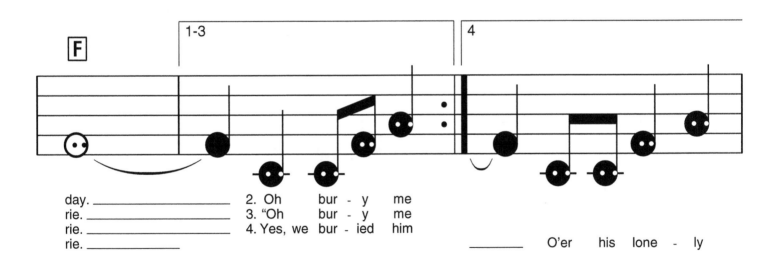

F   1-3   4

day. _____ 2. Oh bur - y me
rie. _____ 3. "Oh bur - y me
rie. _____ 4. Yes, we bur - ied him
rie. _____

_____ O'er his lone - ly

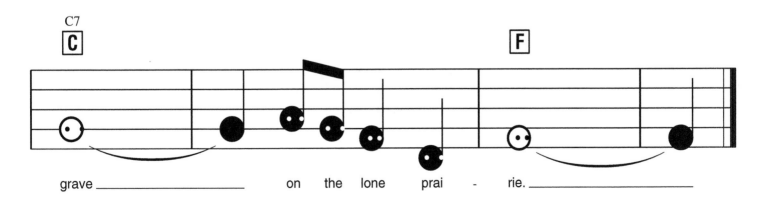

C7
C   F

grave _____ on the lone prai - rie. _____

Dear Old Western Skies

Registration 8
Rhythm: Waltz

Words and Music by
Gene Autry

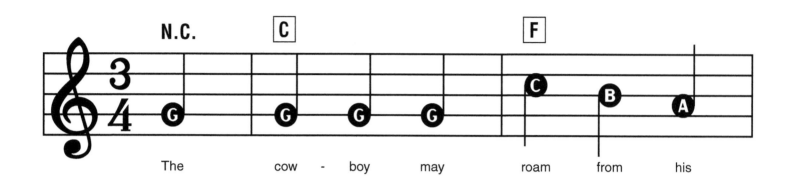

The cow-boy may roam from his

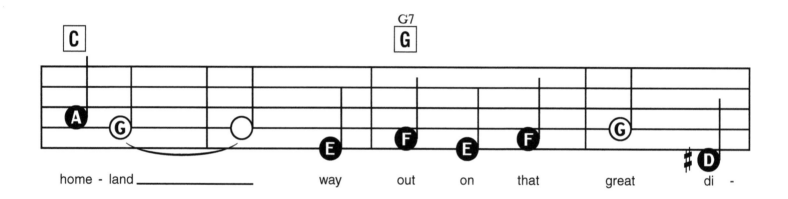

home-land _____ way out on that great di-

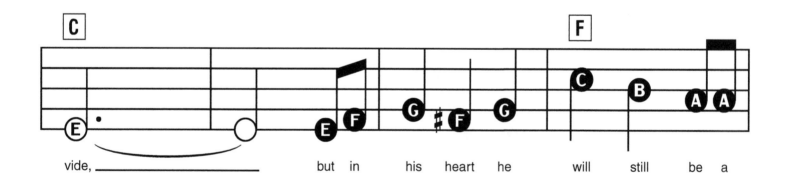

vide, _____ but in his heart he will still be a

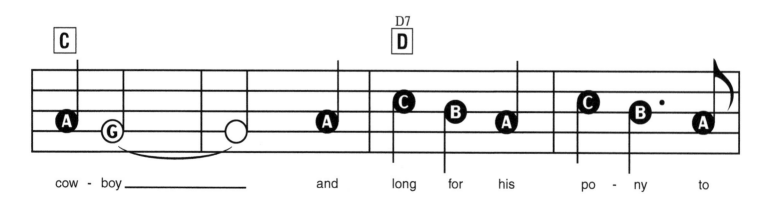

cow-boy _____ and long for his po-ny to

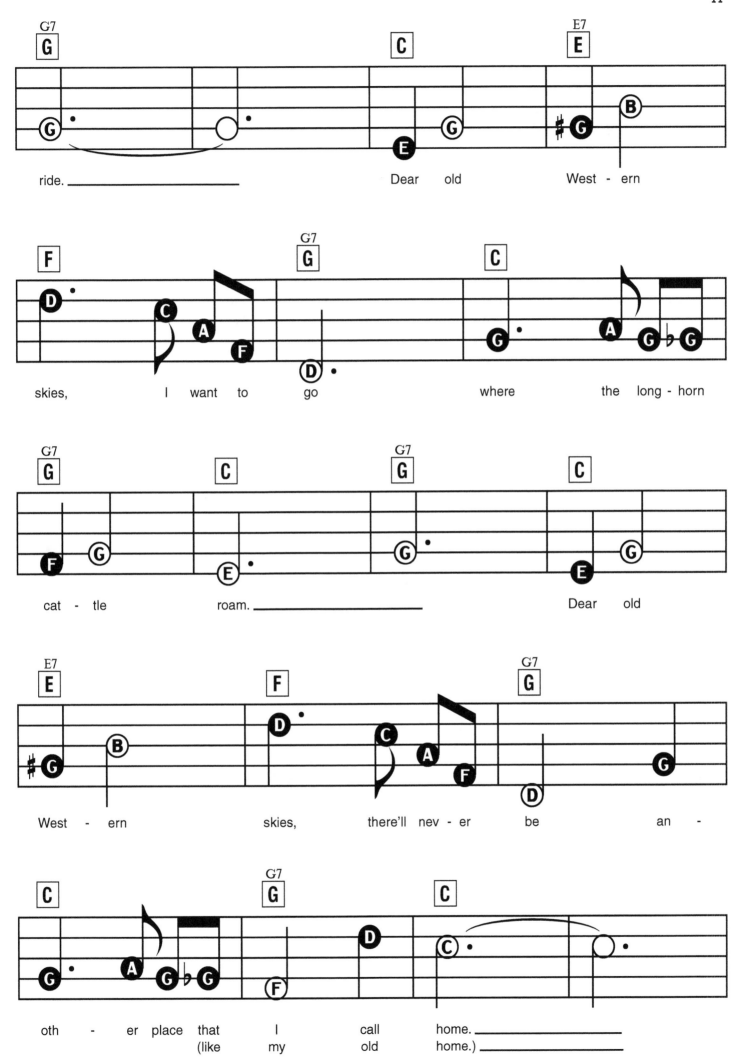

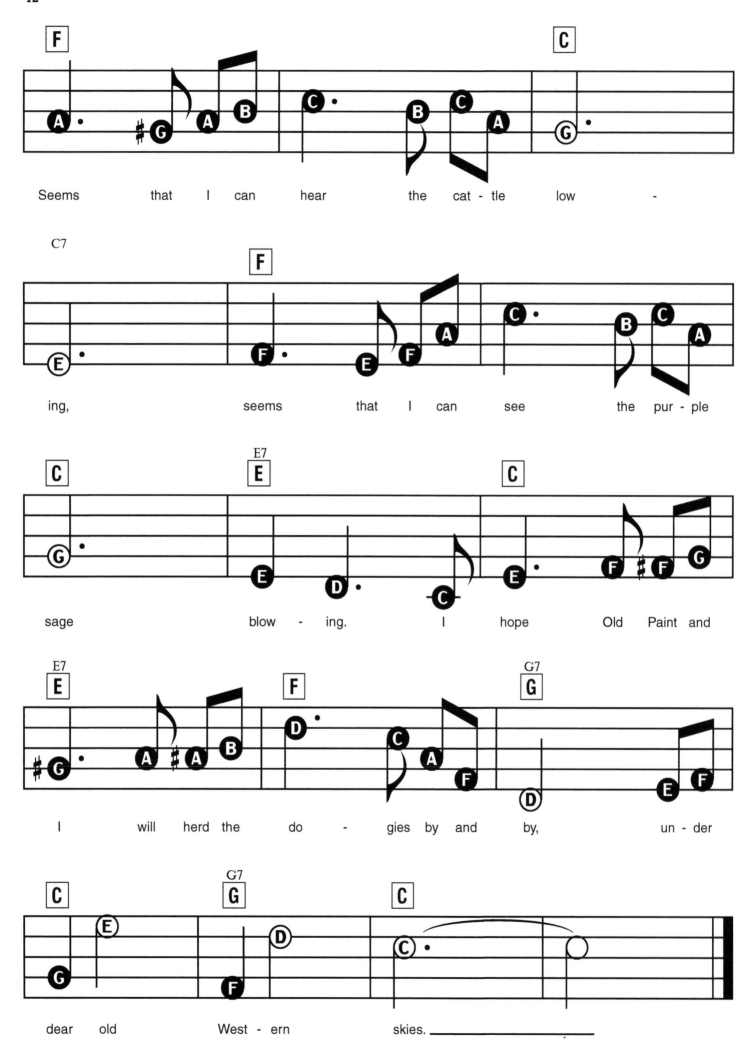

Happy Trails
from the Television Series THE ROY ROGERS SHOW

Registration 5
Rhythm: Swing or Pops

Words and Music by
Dale Evans

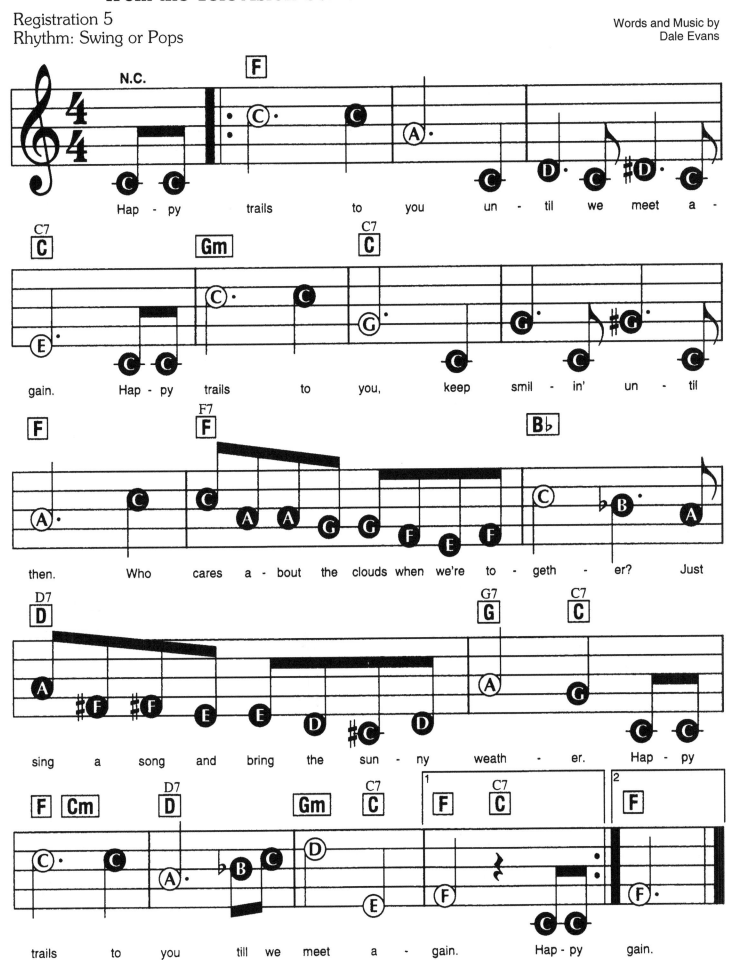

Don't Take Your Guns to Town

Registration 4
Rhythm: Country Western or Fox Trot

Words and Music by
Johnny R. Cash

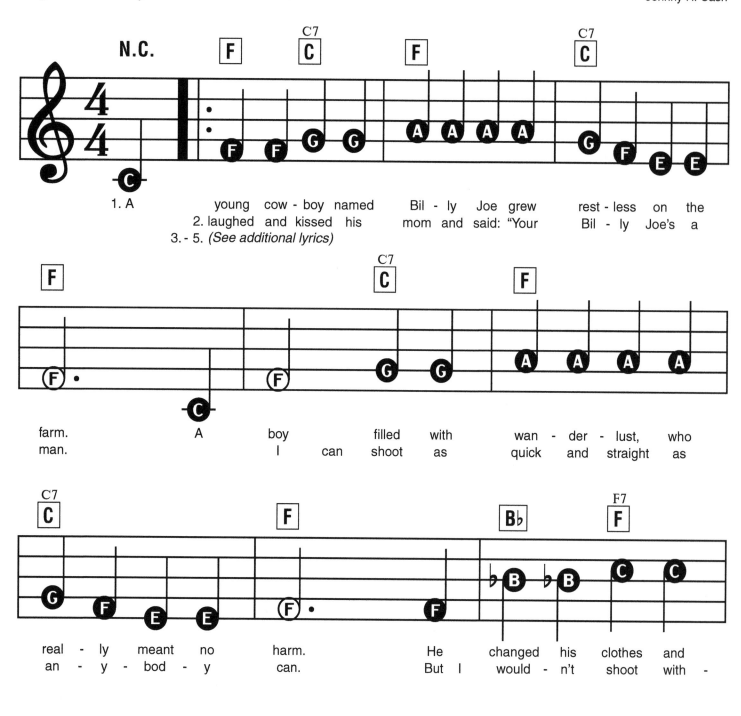

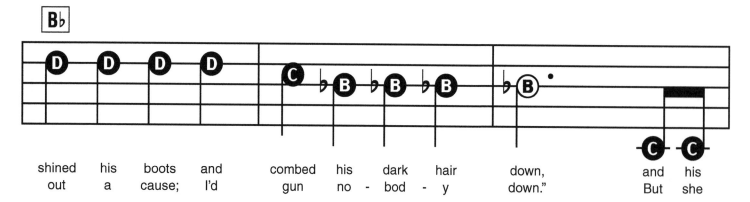

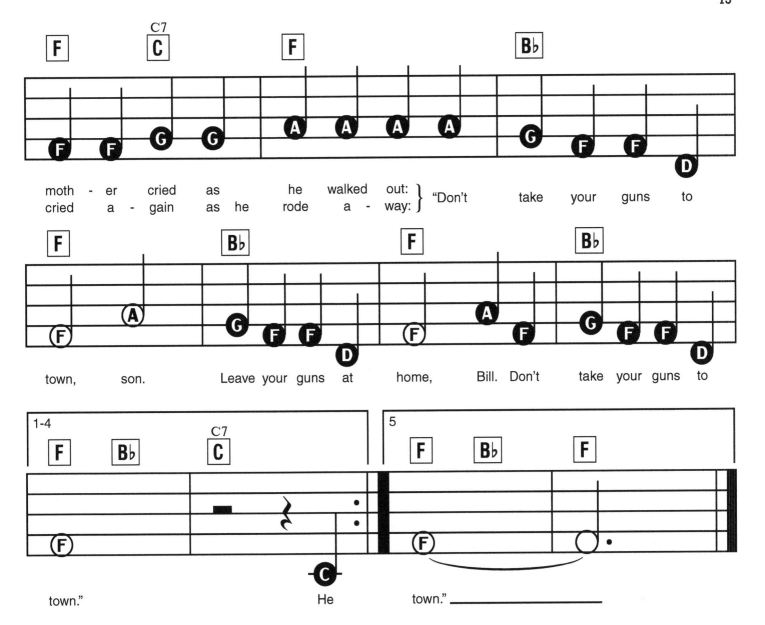

F   C7   C   F   B♭

F   F   G   G   A   A   A   A   G   F   F   D

moth - er   cried   as   he   walked   out: } "Don't   take   your   guns   to

cried   a - gain   as   he   rode   a - way: }

F   B♭   F   B♭

F   A   G   F   F   D   F   A   F   G   F   F   D

town,   son.   Leave   your   guns   at   home,   Bill.   Don't   take   your   guns   to

1-4   F   B♭   C7   C   5   F   B♭   F

F   C   F

town."   He   town." _____

Additional Lyrics

3. He sang a song as on he rode, his guns hung at his hips.
   He rode into a cattle town, a smile upon his lips.
   He stopped and walked into a bar and laid his money down,
   But his mother's words echoed again: "Don't take your guns to town, son.
   Leave your guns at home, Bill. Don't take your guns to town."

4. He drank his first strong liquor then to calm his shaking hand,
   And tried to tell himself at last he had become a man.
   A dusty cowpoke at his side began to laugh him down.
   And he heard again his mother's words: "Don't take your guns to town, son.
   Leave your guns at home, Bill. Don't take your guns to town."

5. Bill was raged and Billy Joe reached for his gun to draw,
   But the stranger drew his gun and fired before he even saw.
   As Billy Joe fell to the floor the crowd all gathered 'round
   And wondered at his final words: "Don't take your guns to town, son.
   Leave your guns at home, Bill. Don't take your guns to town."

Git Along, Little Dogies

Registration 3
Rhythm: Waltz

Collected, Adapted and Arranged by
John A. Lomax and Alan Lomax

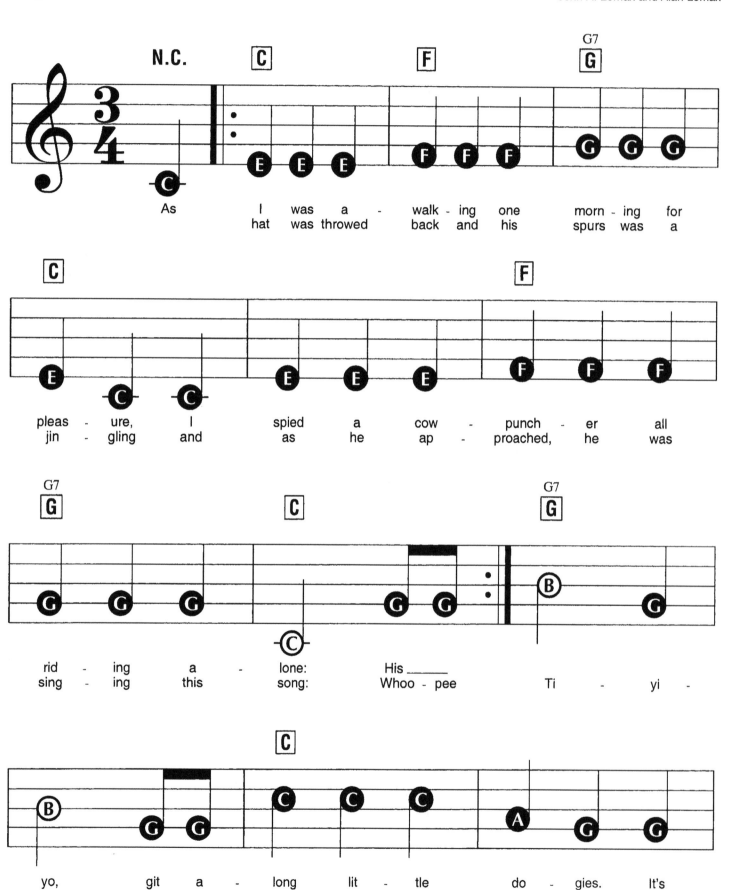

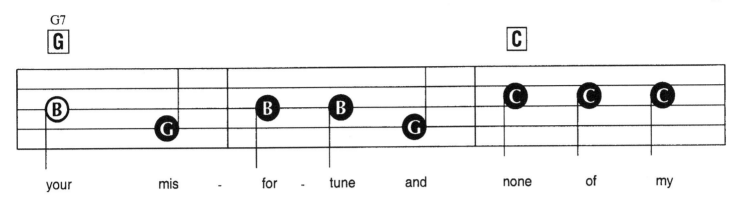

your mis - for - tune and none of my

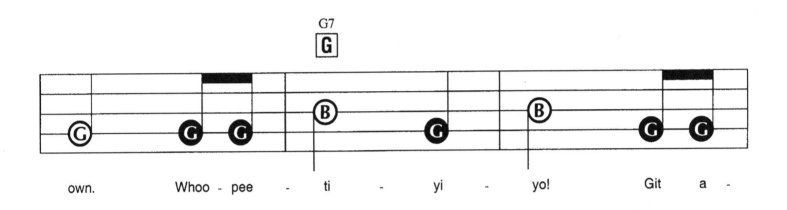

own. Whoo - pee - ti - yi - yo! Git a -

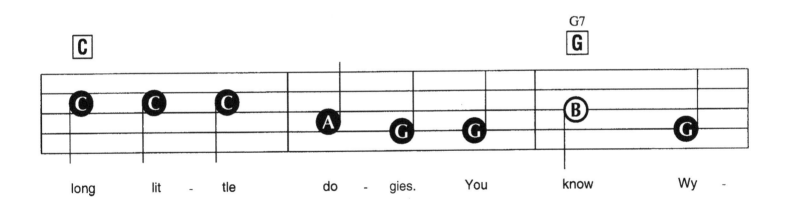

long lit - tle do - gies. You know Wy -

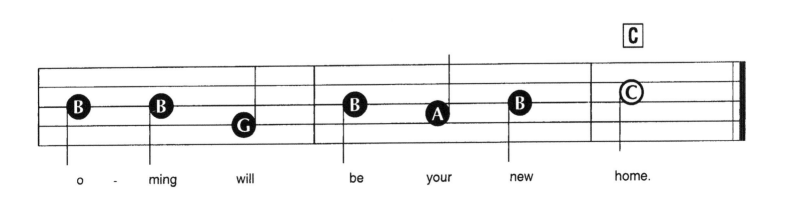

o - ming will be your new home.

High Noon
(Do Not Forsake Me)
from HIGH NOON

Registration 4
Rhythm: Fox Trot

Words and Music by Dimitri Tiomkin
and Ned Washington

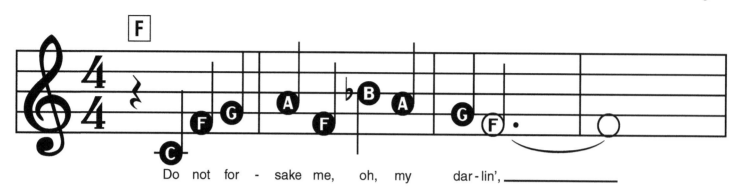

Do not for - sake me, oh, my dar - lin', _____

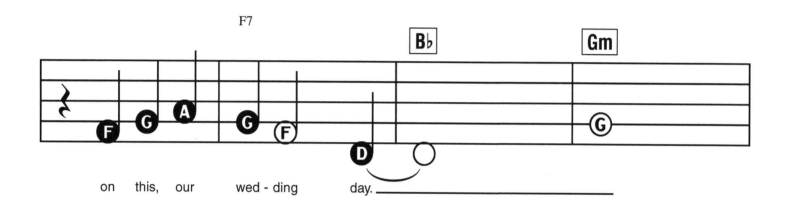

on this, our wed - ding day. _____

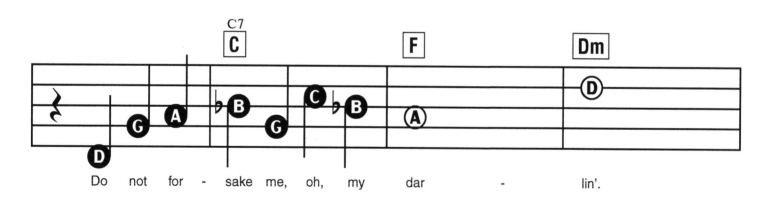

Do not for - sake me, oh, my dar - lin'.

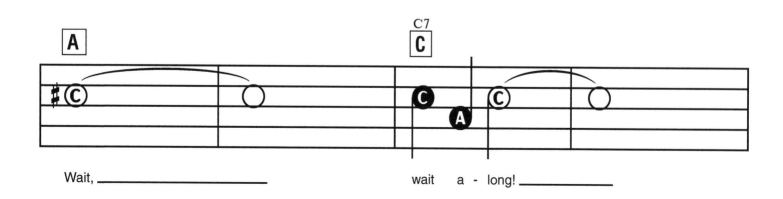

Wait, _____ wait a - long! _____

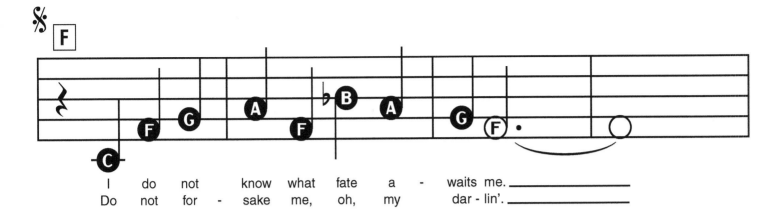

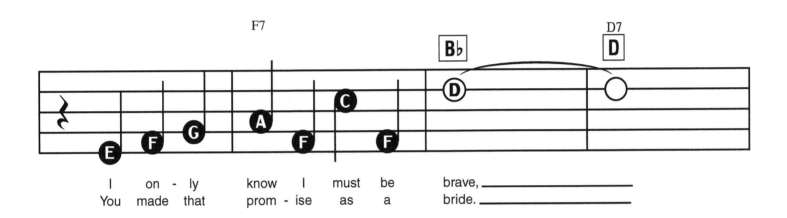

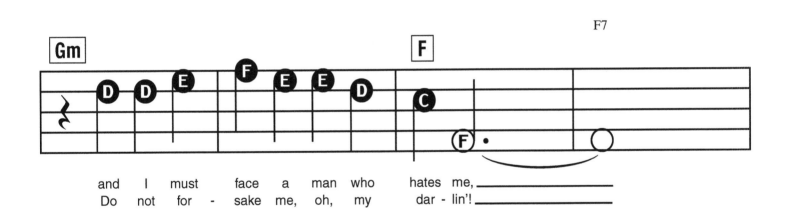

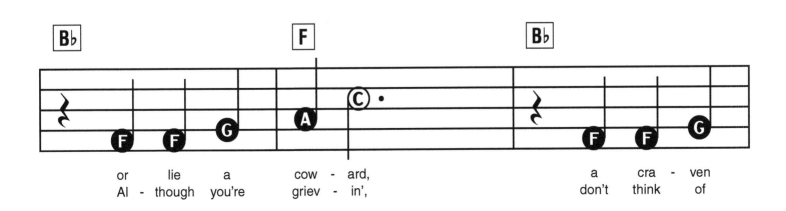

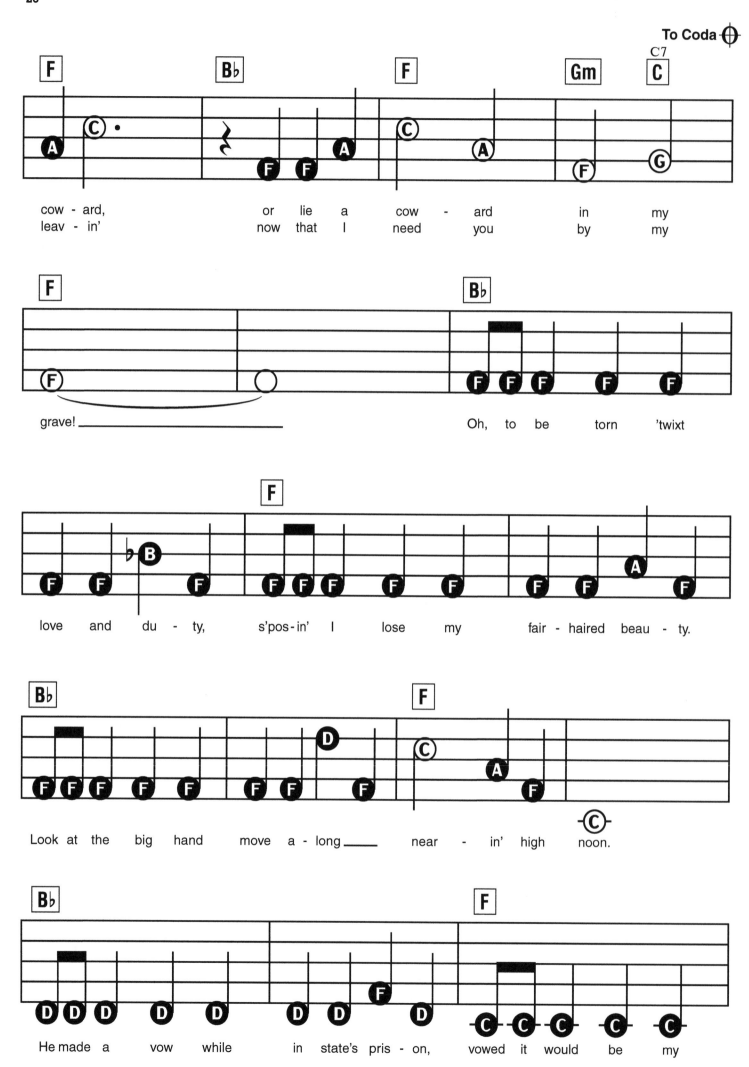

To Coda

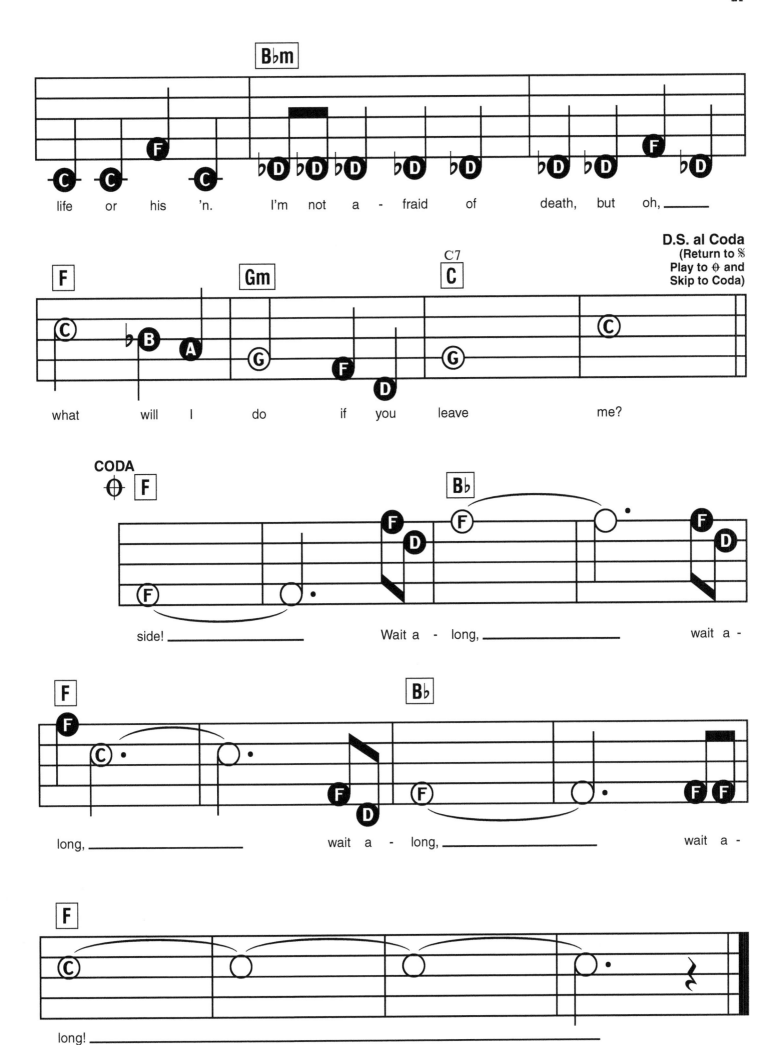

Home on the Range

Registration 4
Rhythm: Waltz

Lyrics by Dr. Brewster Higley
Music by Dan Kelly

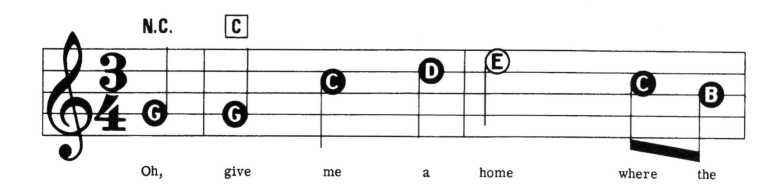

Oh, give me a home where the

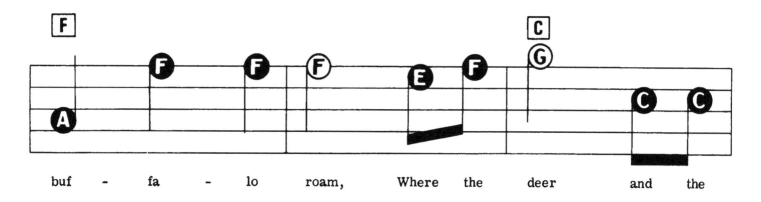

buf - fa - lo roam, Where the deer and the

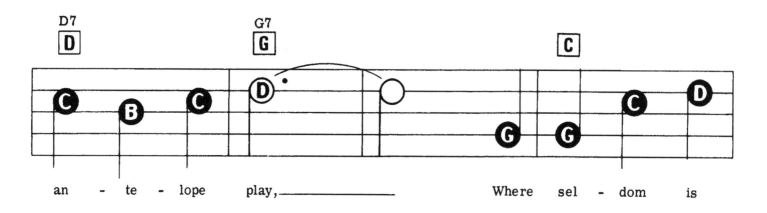

an - te - lope play,_____ Where sel - dom is

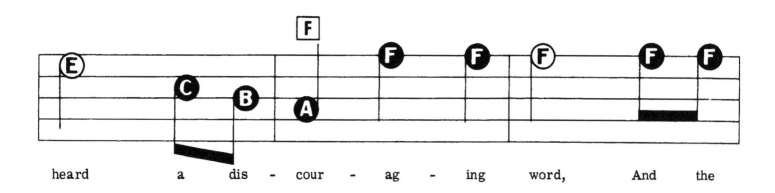

heard a dis - cour - ag - ing word, And the

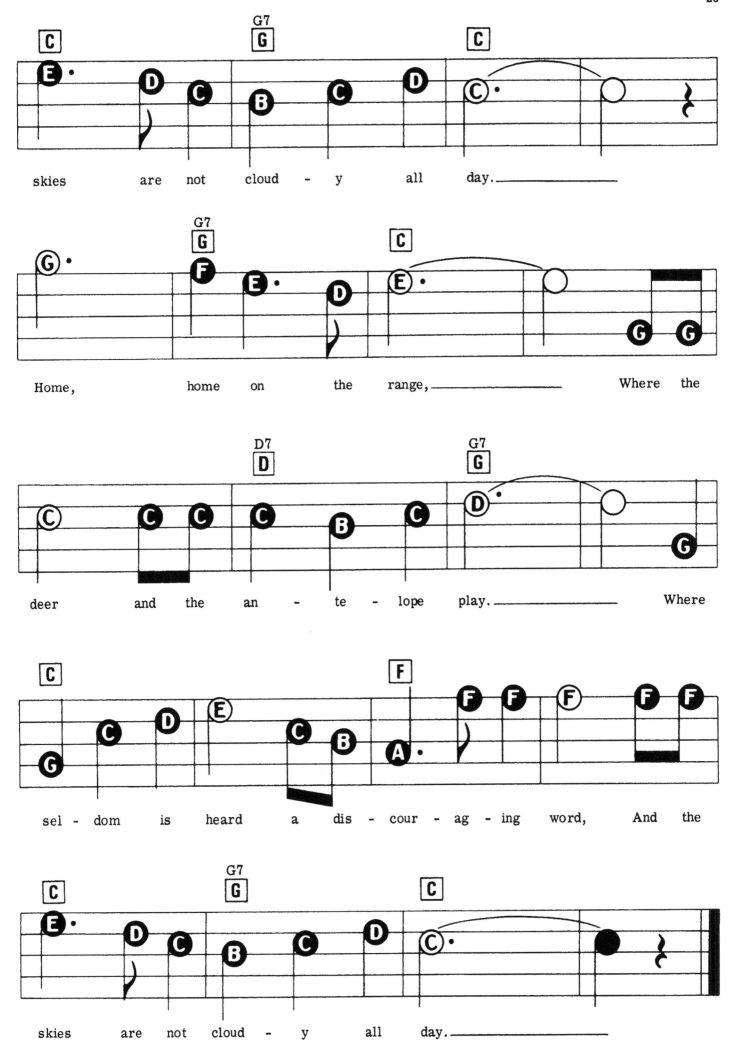

Jingle Jangle Jingle
(I Got Spurs)
from the Paramount Picture THE FOREST RANGERS

Registration 4
Rhythm: Country or Swing

Words by Frank Loesser
Music by Joseph J. Lilley

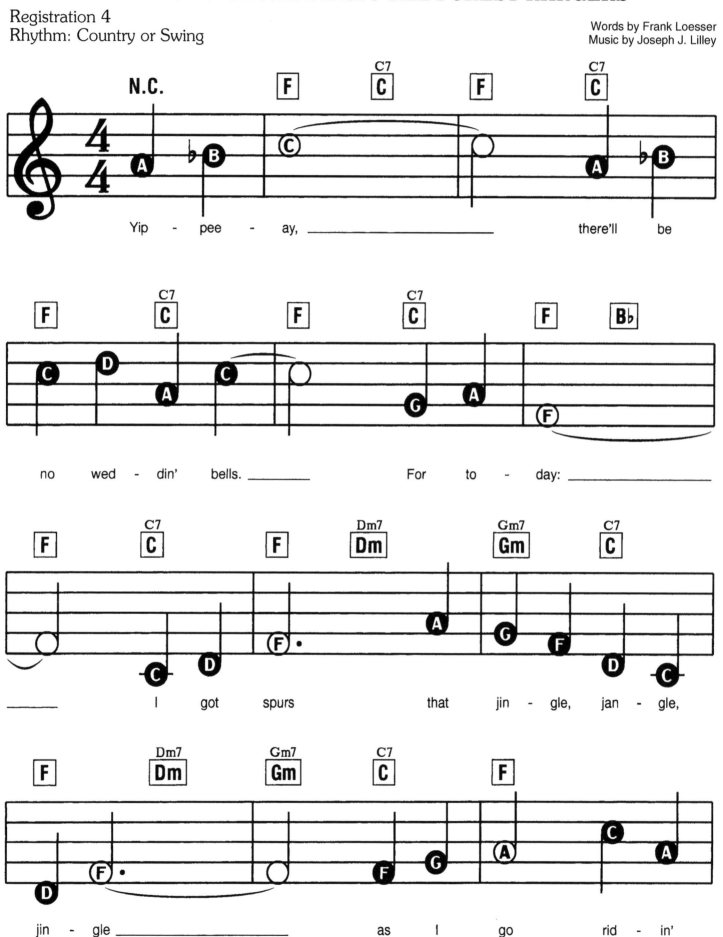

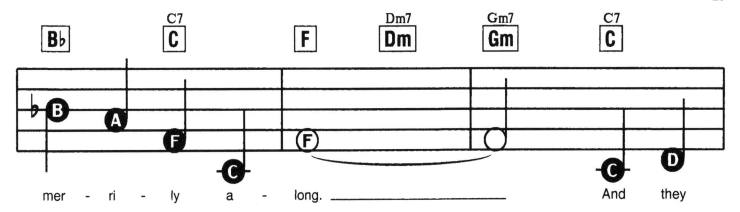

mer - ri - ly a - long. _____ And they

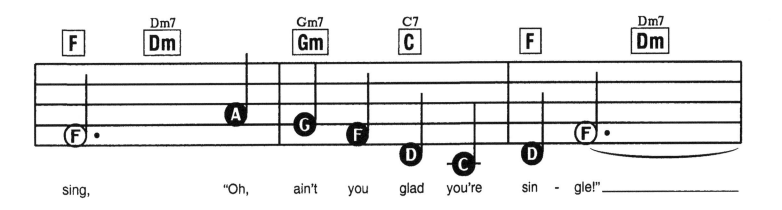

sing, "Oh, ain't you glad you're sin - gle!" _____

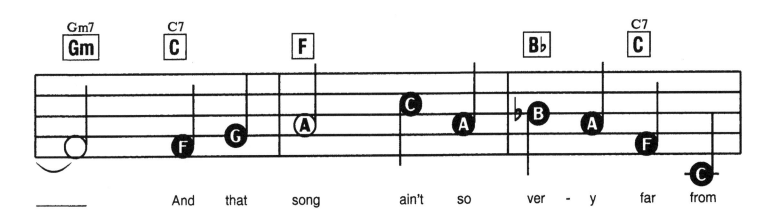

_____ And that song ain't so ver - y far from

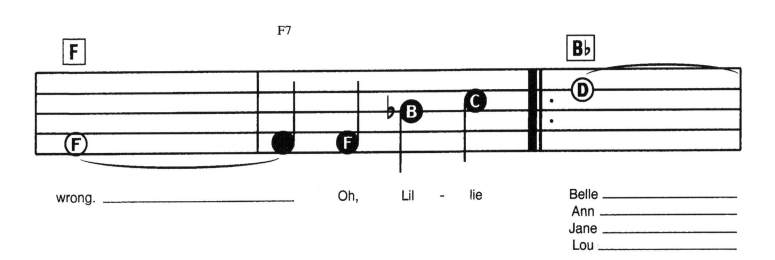

wrong. _____ Oh, Lil - lie

Belle _____
Ann _____
Jane _____
Lou _____

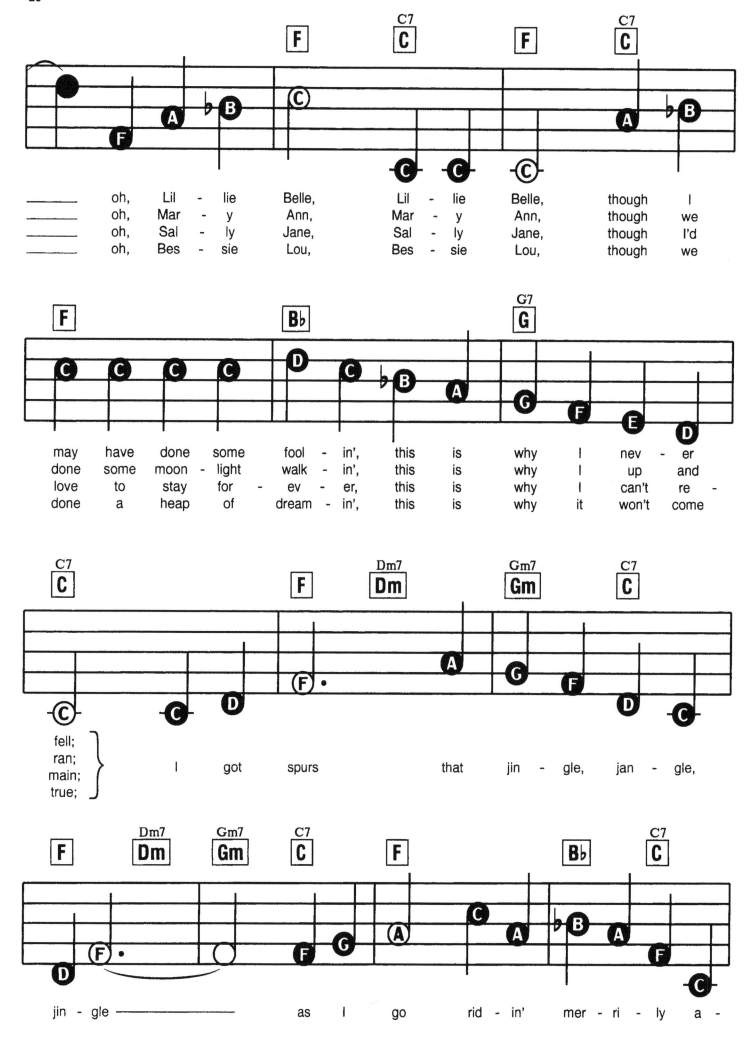

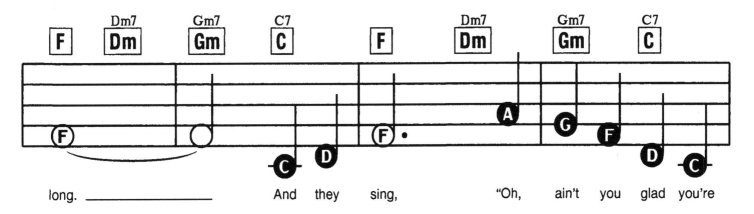

long. _____ And they sing, "Oh, ain't you glad you're

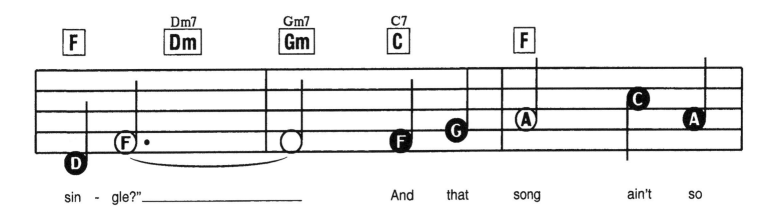

sin - gle?"_____ And that song ain't so

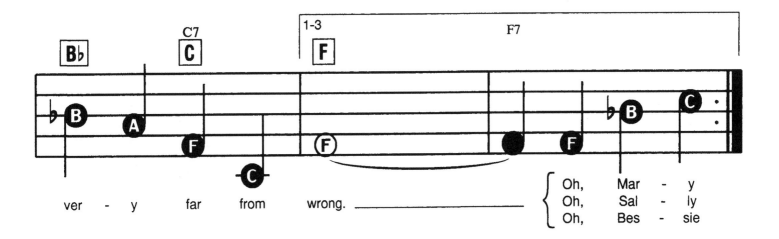

ver - y far from wrong. _____

Oh, Mar - y
Oh, Sal - ly
Oh, Bes - sie

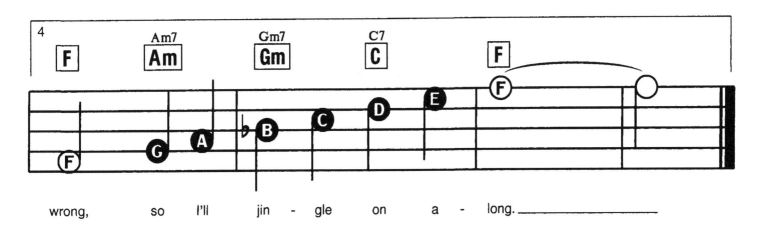

wrong, so I'll jin - gle on a - long._____

Mexicali Rose
from MEXICALI ROSE

Registration 3
Rhythm: Waltz

Words by Helen Stone
Music by Jack B. Tenney

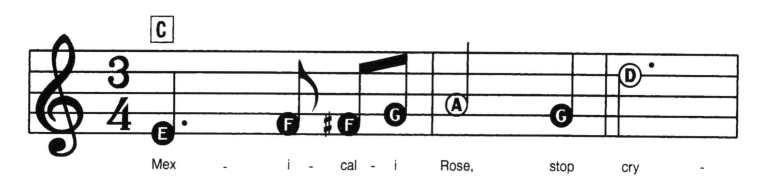

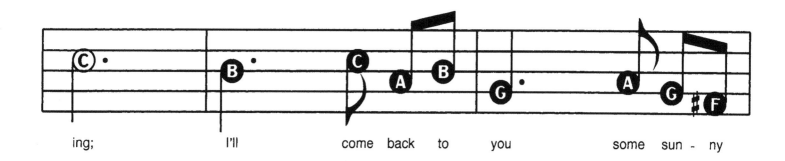

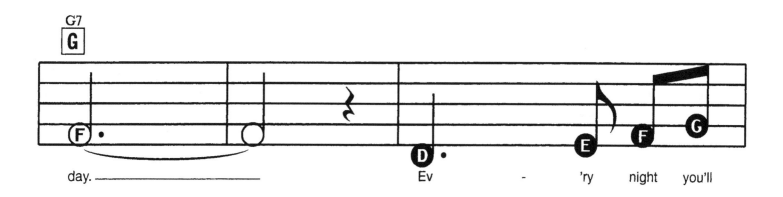

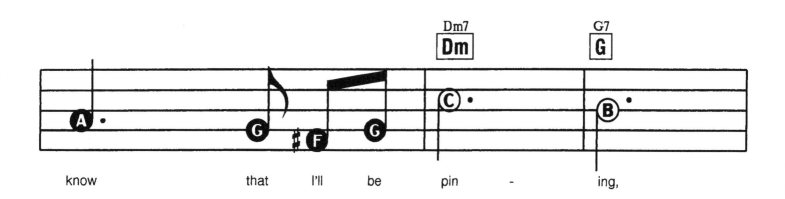

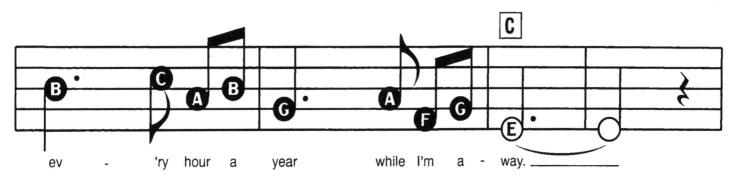

ev - 'ry hour a year while I'm a - way. ____

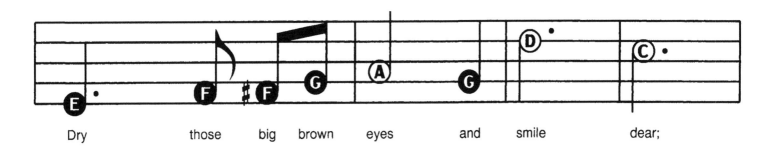

Dry those big brown eyes and smile dear;

C7

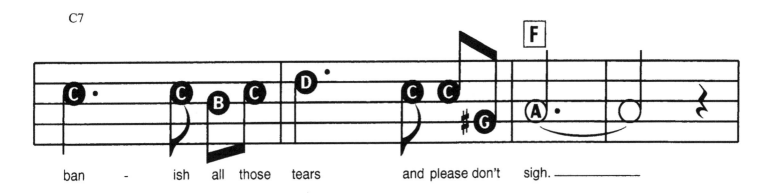

ban - ish all those tears and please don't sigh. ____

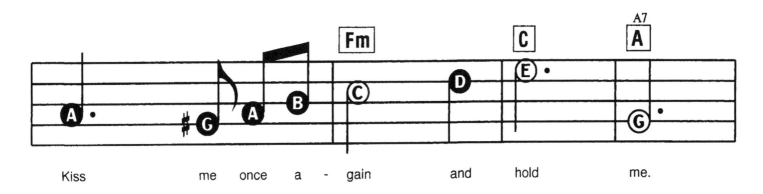

Kiss me once a - gain and hold me.

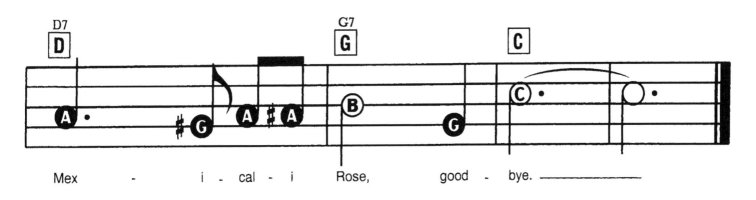

Mex - i - cal - i Rose, good - bye. ____

Mule Train

Registration 2
Rhythm: Country Swing or Fox Trot

Words and Music by Johnny Lange,
Hy Heath and Fred Glickman

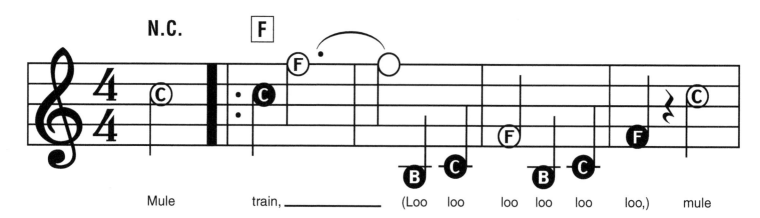

Mule   train, _____   (Loo   loo   loo   loo   loo   loo,)   mule

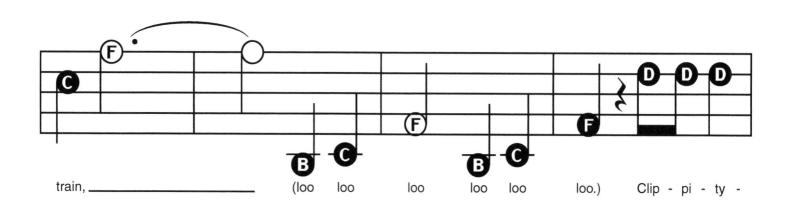

train, _____   (loo   loo   loo   loo   loo   loo.)   Clip - pi - ty -

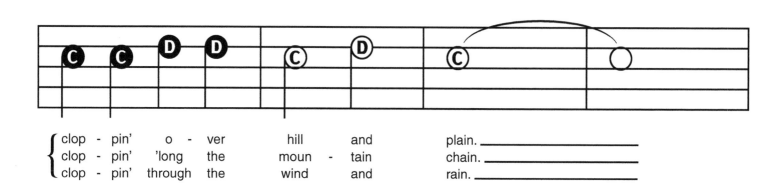

{ clop - pin' o - ver   hill   and   plain. _____
{ clop - pin' 'long the   moun - tain   chain. _____
{ clop - pin' through the wind and   rain. _____

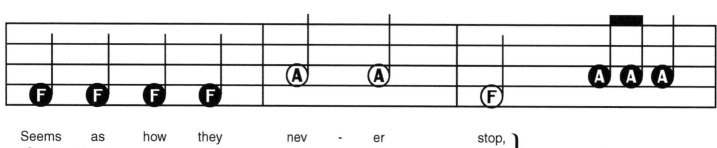

Seems   as   how   they   nev - er   stop, }
Soon they're gon - na   reach   the   top, }   clip - pi - ty -
They'll keep go - in'   till   they   drop, }

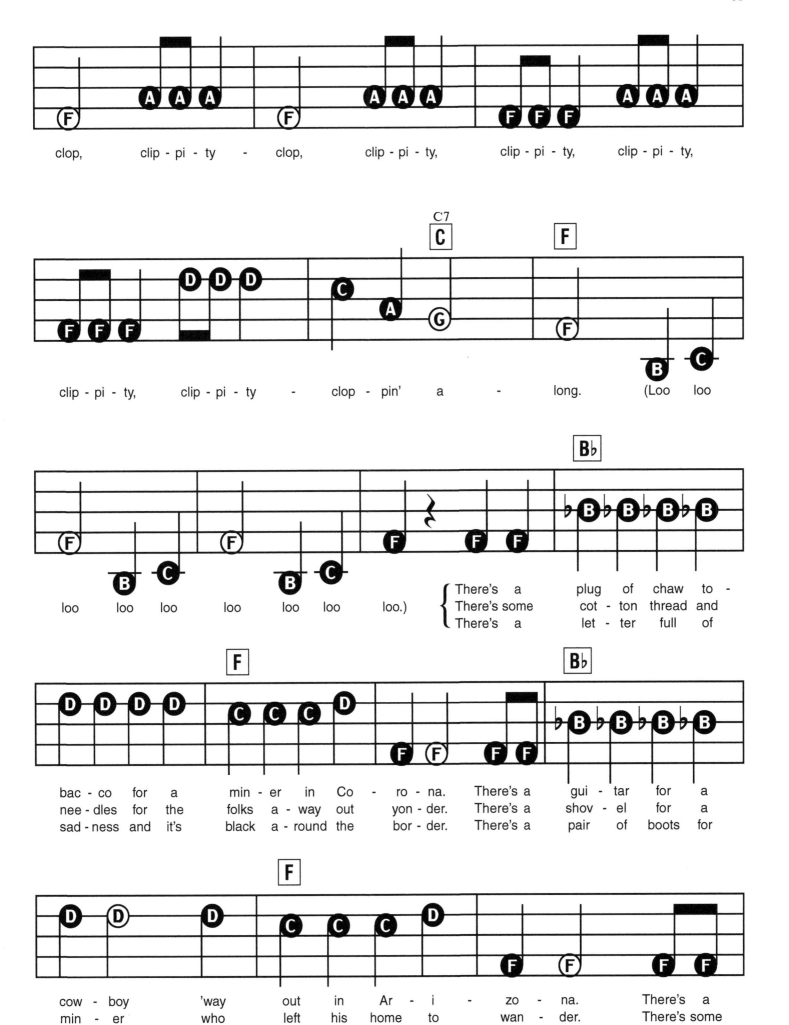

32

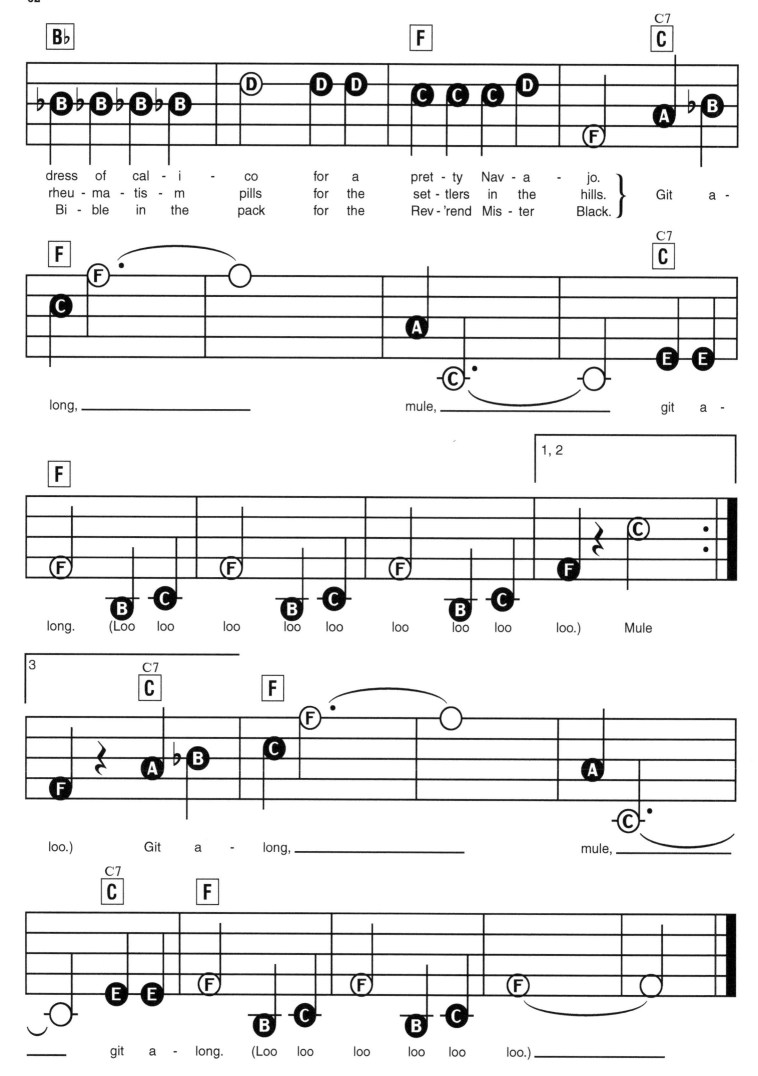

dress of cal - i - co   for   a   pret - ty Nav - a - jo.
rheu - ma - tis - m   pills   for   the   set - tlers   in   the   hills.   Git a -
Bi - ble   in   the   pack   for   the   Rev - 'rend Mis - ter   Black.

long, _____   mule, _____   git a -

long. (Loo loo   loo   loo loo   loo   loo loo   loo.)   Mule

loo.)   Git a - long, _____   mule, _____

_____   git a - long. (Loo loo   loo   loo loo   loo.) _____

(Ghost)
Riders in the Sky
(A Cowboy Legend)
from RIDERS IN THE SKY

Registration 10
Rhythm: March or Polka

By Stan Jones

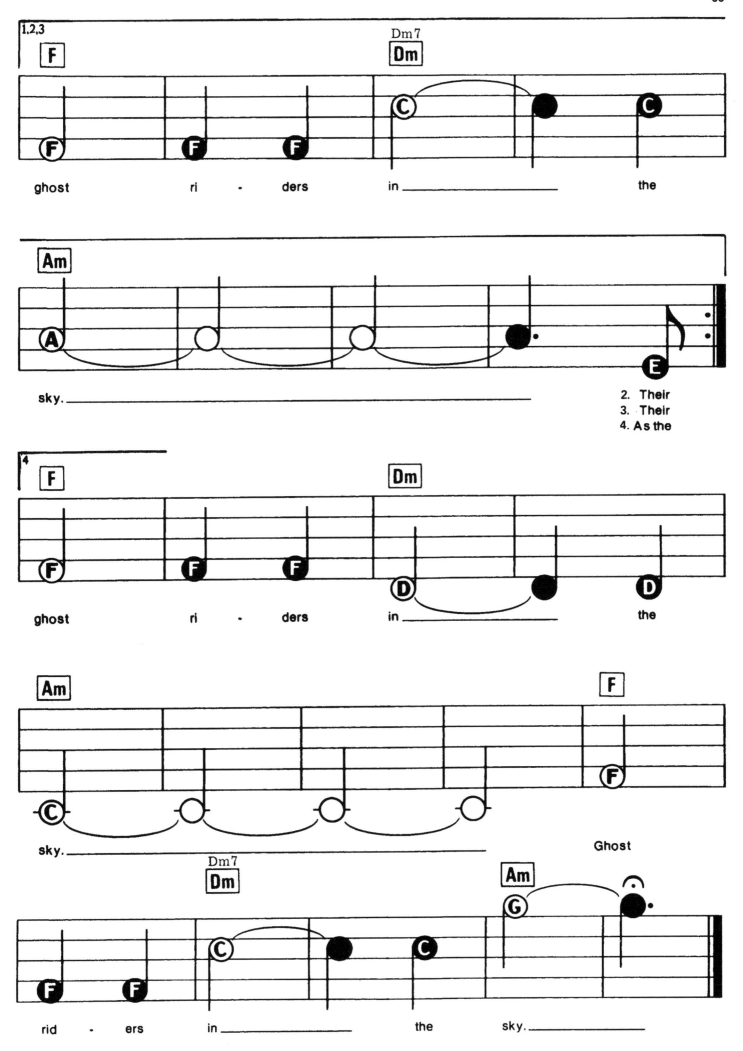

The Old Chisholm Trail

Registration 8
Rhythm: Country or Fox Trot

Texas Cowboy Song

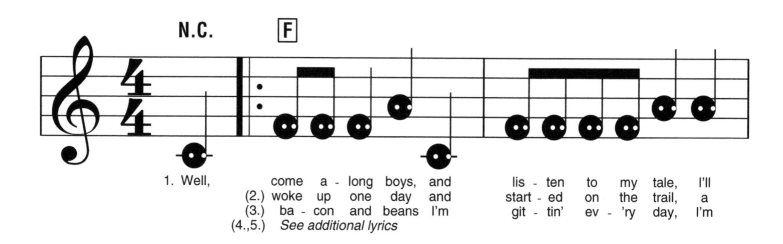

1. Well, come a-long boys, and lis-ten to my tale, I'll
(2.) woke up one day and start-ed on the trail, a
(3.) ba-con and beans I'm git-tin' ev-'ry day, I'm
(4.,5.) *See additional lyrics*

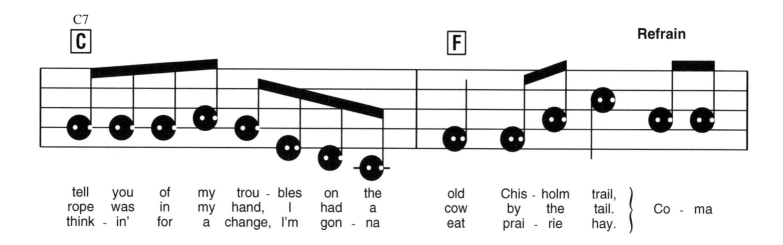

tell you of my trou-bles on the old Chis-holm trail,
rope was in my hand, I had a cow by the tail. } Co - ma
think-in' for a change, I'm gon-na eat prai-rie hay.

Refrain

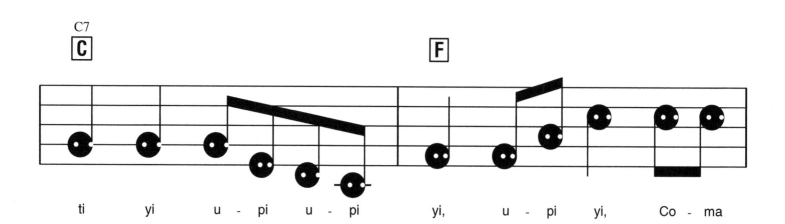

ti yi u-pi u-pi yi, u-pi yi, Co - ma

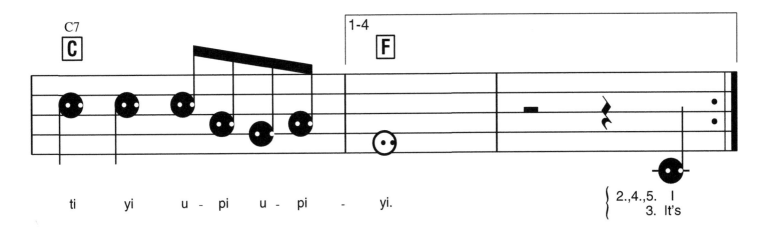

ti   yi   u - pi   u - pi -   yi.

{ 2.,4.,5. I
  3. It's

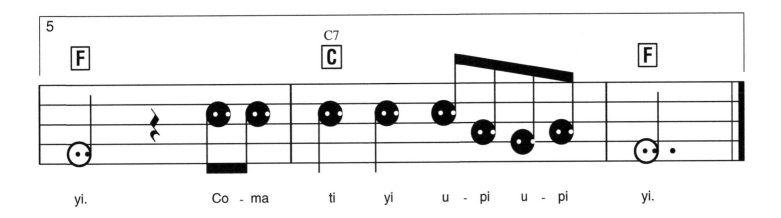

yi.   Co - ma   ti   yi   u - pi   u - pi   yi.

Additional Lyrics

3. I went to the boss for pickin' up my roll,
   He figured what I borrowed, I was nine in the hole.
   Refrain

4. I guess I must wait till I'm old enough to die,
   I'll quit a-punching cattle in the sweet by and by.
   Refrain

The Red River Valley

Registration 4
Rhythm: Swing

Traditional American Cowboy Song

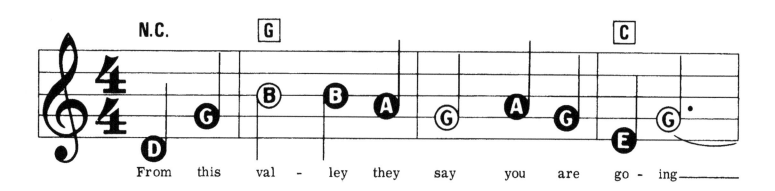

From this val - ley they say you are go - ing

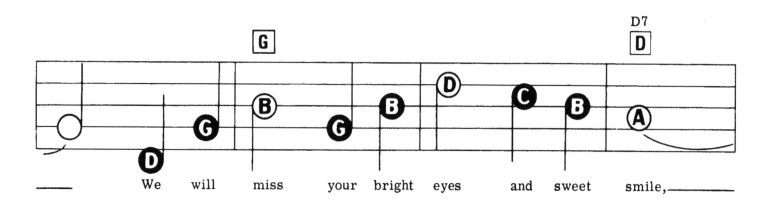

We will miss your bright eyes and sweet smile,

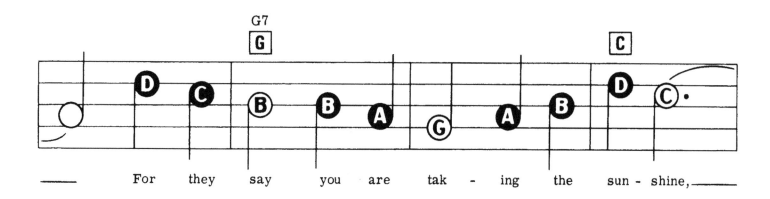

For they say you are tak - ing the sun - shine,

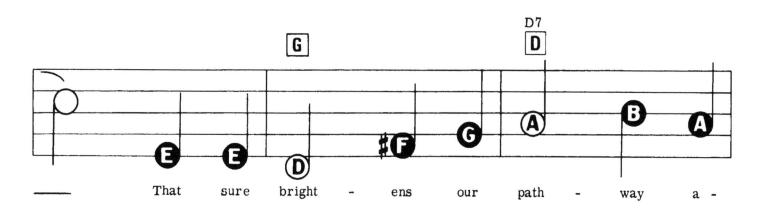

That sure bright - ens our path - way a -

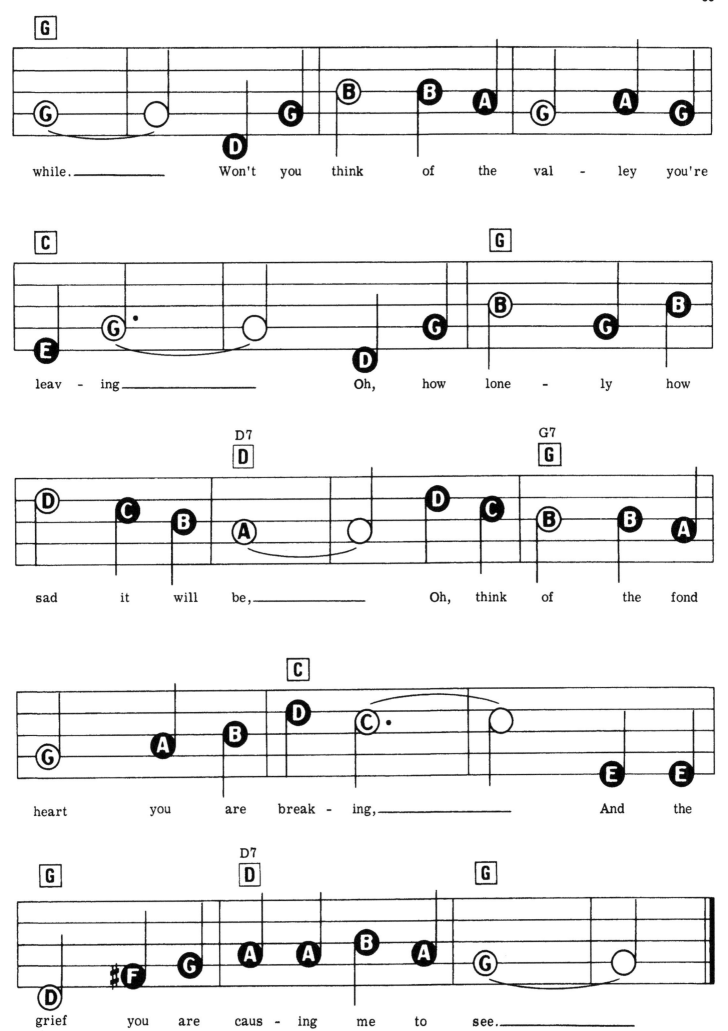

Streets of Laredo
(The Cowboy's Lament)

Registration 3
Rhythm: Waltz

Collected, Adapted and Arranged by
John A. Lomax and Alan Lomax

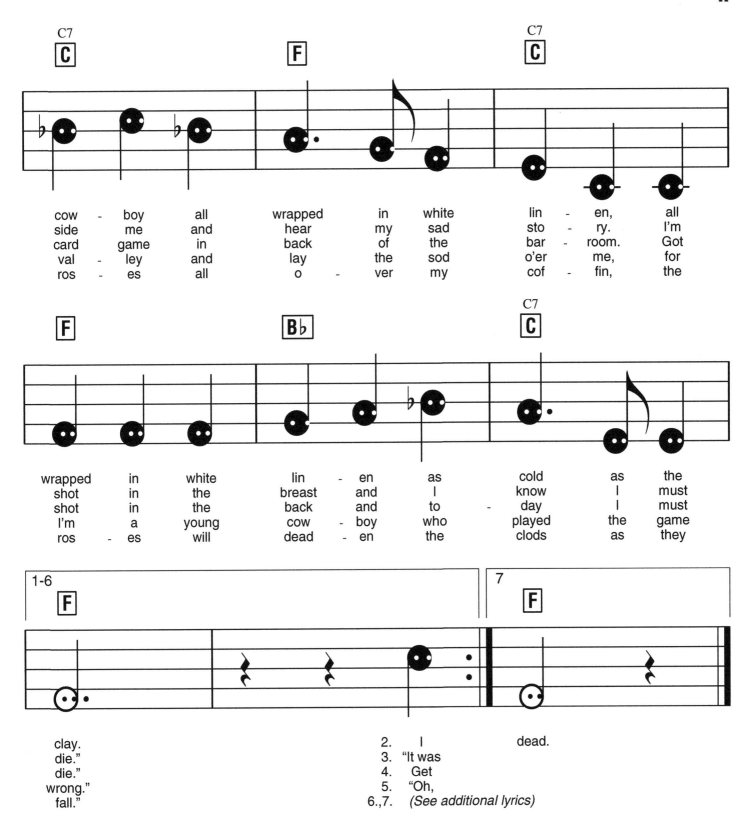

cow - boy all wrapped in white lin - en, all
side me and hear my sad sto - ry. I'm
card game in back of the bar - room. Got
val - ley and lay the sod o'er me, for
ros - es all o - ver my cof - fin, the

wrapped in white lin - en as cold as the
shot in the breast and know day I must
shot in the back and to - day I must
I'm a young cow - boy who played the game
ros - es will dead - en the clods as they

1-6

clay.
die."
die."
wrong."
fall."

7

2. I dead.
3. "It was
4. Get
5. "Oh,
6.,7. *(See additional lyrics)*

Additional Lyrics

6. "Go gather around you a crowd of young cowboys,
And tell them the story of this my sad fate.
Tell one and the other before they go further,
To stop their wild roving before it's too late."

7. "Go fetch me a cup, just a cup of cold water,
To cool my parched lips," the cowboy then said.
Before I returned, his brave spirit had left him,
And, gone to his Maker, the cowboy was dead.

Take Me Back to My Boots and Saddle

Registration 2
Rhythm: Country Swing or Fox Trot

Words and Music by Walter Samuels,
Teddy Powell and Leonard Whitcup

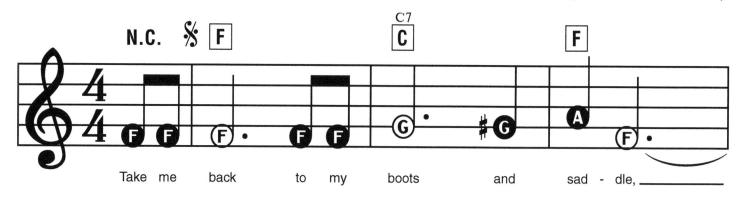

Take me back to my boots and sad - dle, _____

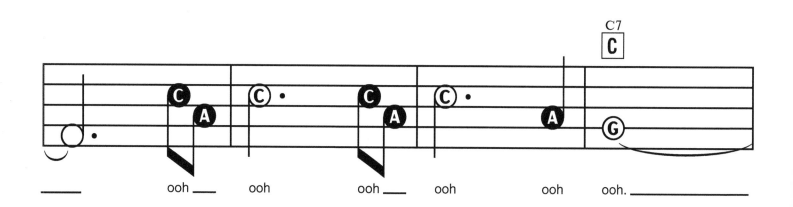

____ ooh ___ ooh ooh ___ ooh ooh ooh. ___

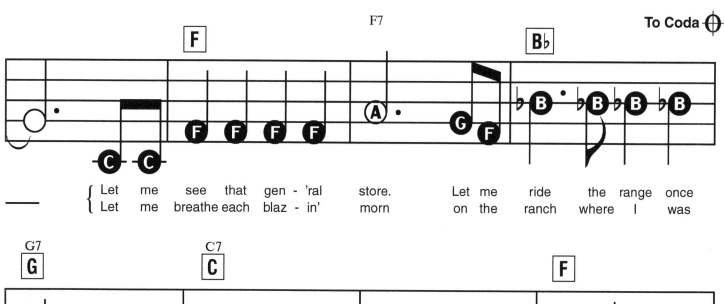

___ { Let me see that gen - 'ral store. Let me ride the range once
      Let me breathe each blaz - in' morn on the ranch where I was

more. Give me my boots and sad - dle. _____

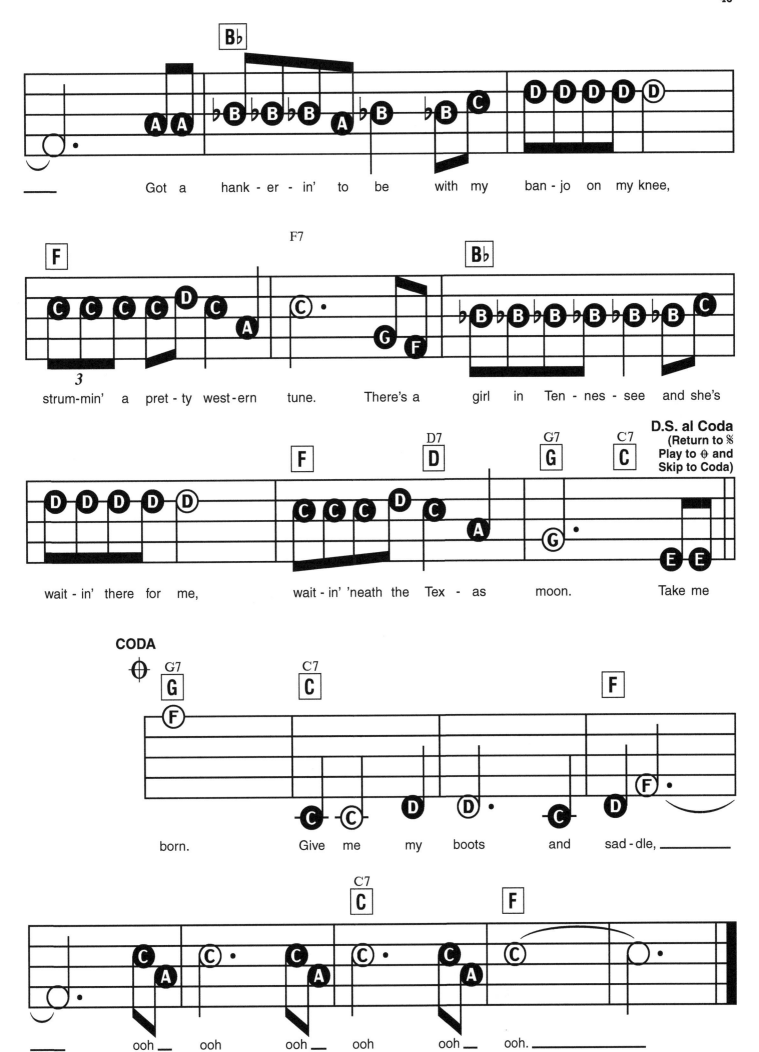

Wagon Wheels

Registration 4
Rhythm: Ballad or Fox Trot

Words by Billy Hill
Music by Peter DeRose

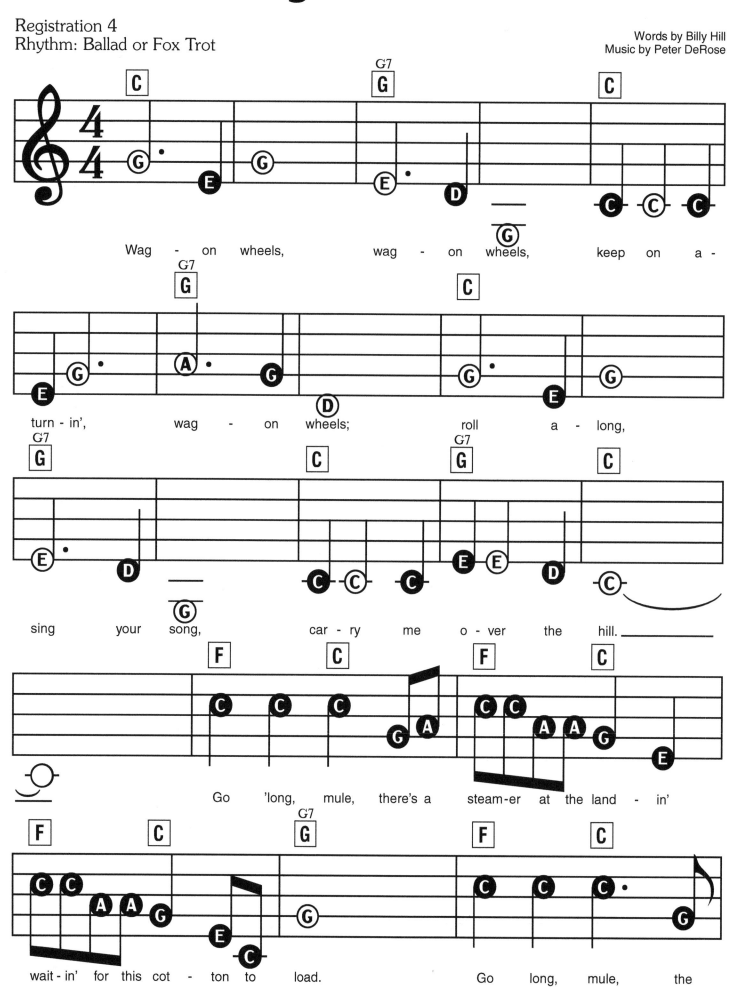

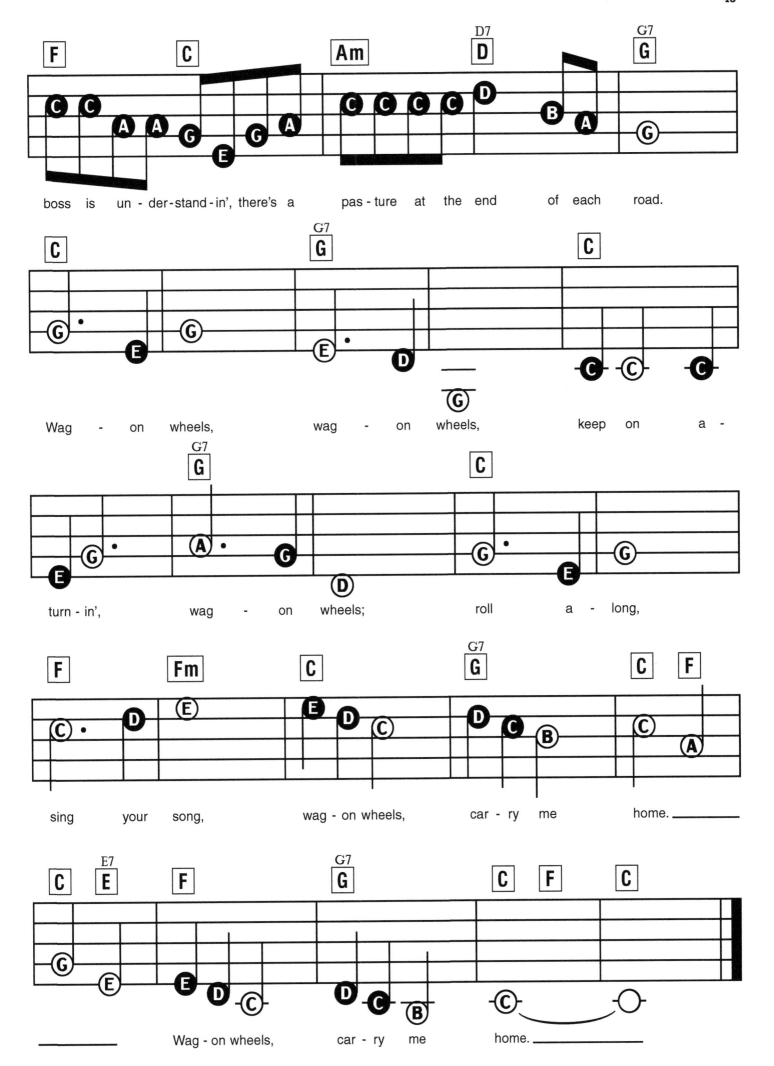

That Silver Haired Daddy of Mine

Registration 8
Rhythm: Country Swing or Fox Trot

Words and Music by Gene Autry
and Jimmy Long

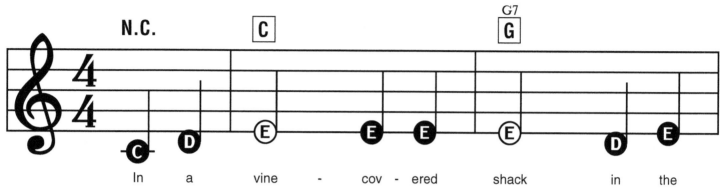

In a vine - cov - ered shack in the

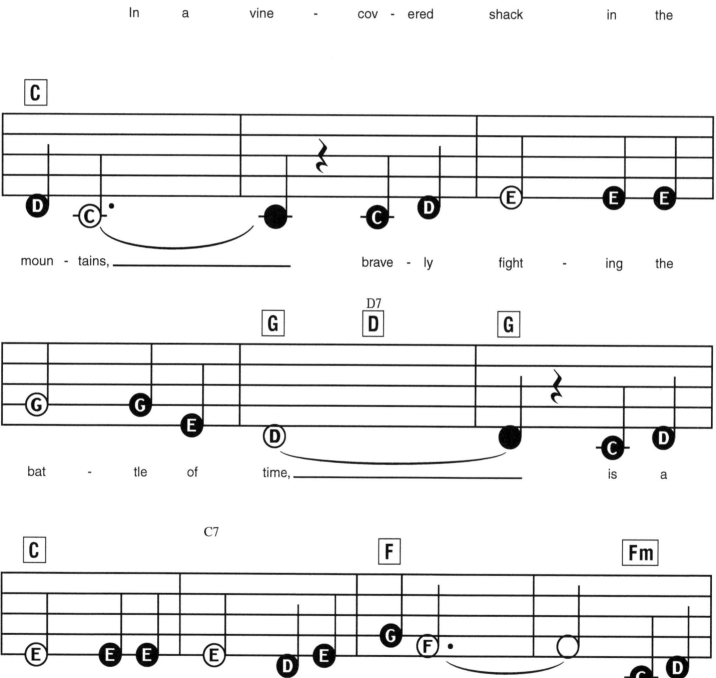

moun - tains, _____ brave - ly fight - ing the

bat - tle of time, _____ is a

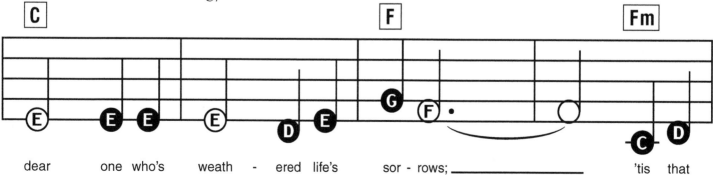

dear one who's weath - ered life's sor - rows; _____ 'tis that

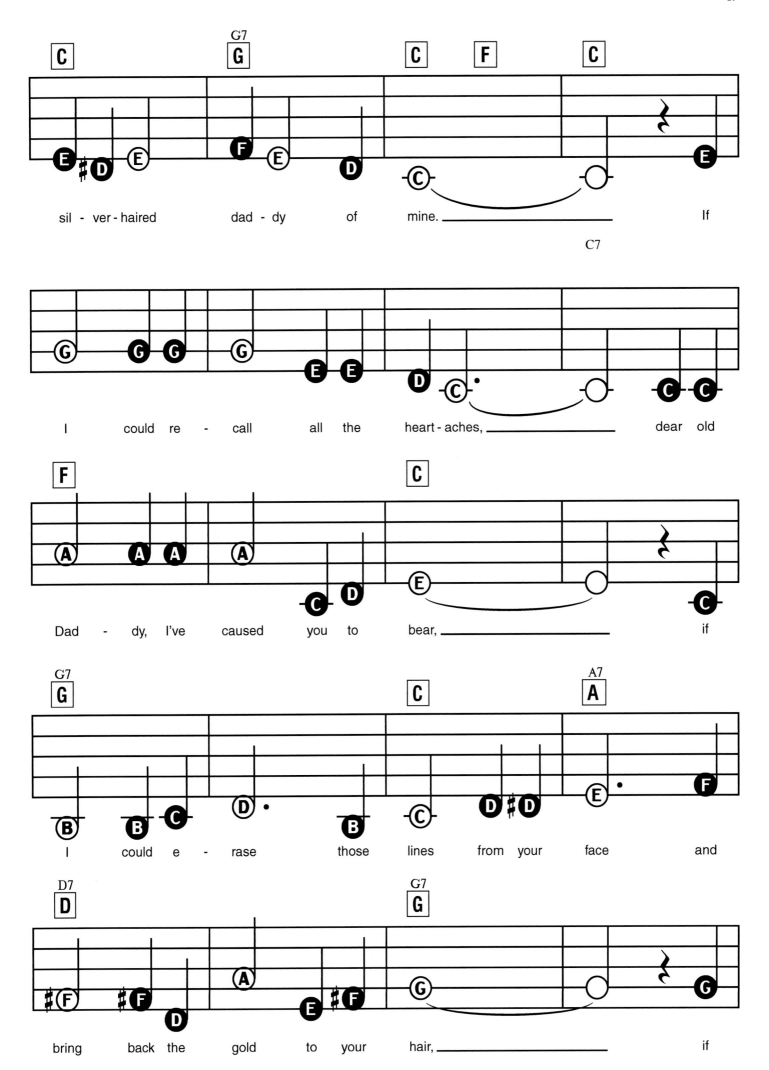

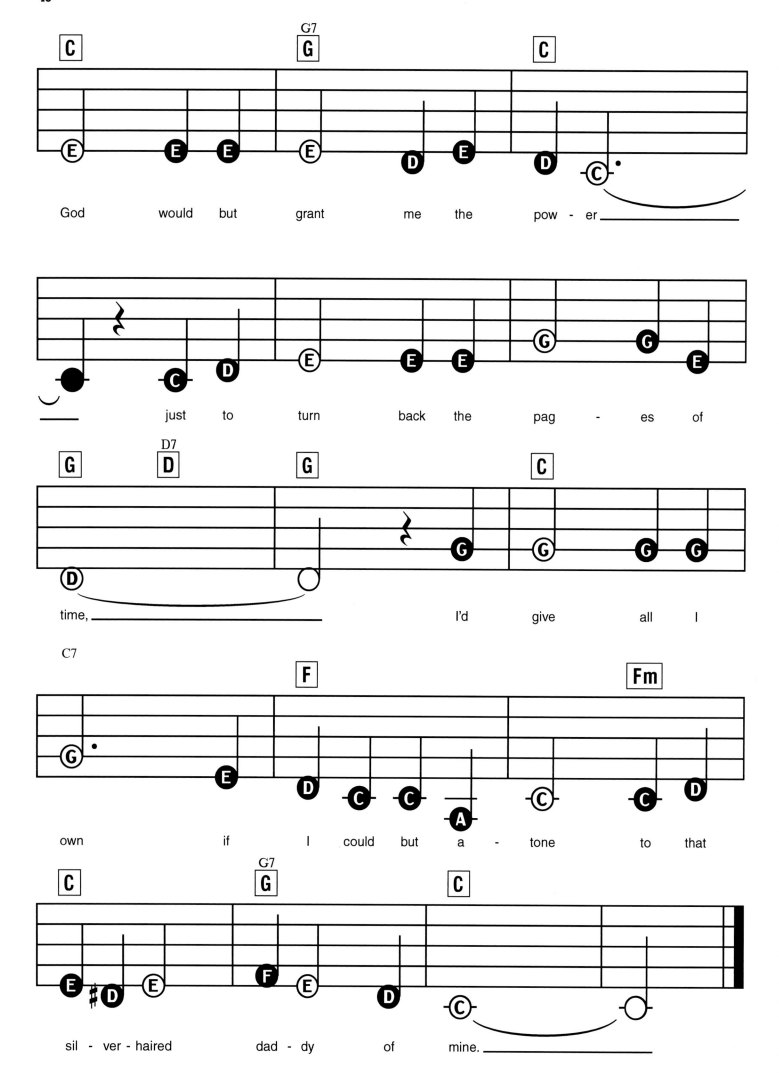